Healing For the Hurting

Karen Stephens Cooper

Sula Too LLC - Publishing
Tampa, Florida

ISBN-978-0-9791560-6-9 (Paperback Edition)
Editor: Candice Williams, Stafford, VA.
Photographers:
  Kyunnie Shuman - CDP Productions
  Carla Brown - CDB Productions
All Bible quotations were taken from the New International Version [NIV]. Definitions taken from *Merriam Webster*

First Printing April 2018
Published by:
Sula Too LLC - Publishing, 5508 N 50th St, Suite 16A Tampa FL 33610
www.sulatoo.com/publishing
Printed in the United States

Healing
For the Hurting

To request volume pricing

(50 copies or more)

and

book Karen S. Cooper

for your next event:

<u>*www.karenstephenscooper.com*</u>

Serenity Living

I come to share

my testimonies through spiritual,

uplifting, unique, self-worth poems,

and short stories.

Dedication

This book is dedicated to:

my daughters - Kalonna, Carla

and

my guardian angel,

Kaylondra

Acknowledgements

Above all things I give God the glory for allowing me to inspire, encourage, give hope and share His love. I thank Him for all I am, and all that I have. Without Him none of this would have been possible.

A special thanks to my dearest friends, Iris, Betty, and Katina who encouraged me along my journey, held my hand and motivated me to step out on faith.

I give my sincere gratitude to my best friend Angie. She opened her home, her heart, and gave my girls and me so much support. She has been truly a honorable friend. Her inspiration saved me from self.

To my mom, my siblings, and my spiritual mothers. Thank you for your roles in my life. Thank you for your love. For I'm a part of you and I will love you always.

To my daughters Kalonna and Carla, my heart strings, my joy. My song bird and my love child. My love for you is God's love for us. My love has no beginning or ending., it's eternal. Thank you for being who you are, and for becoming what God has called you to be. Thank you for giving me hope, and true love.

God has placed me under the guidance of an anointed man of God, Dr. Bishop Matthew M. Odum, Sr. the Shepherd of The Temple of Glory Community Church of Savannah, Georgia. I have been feed, taught and blessed by his teachings. I thank God for him.

Many thanks to Overseer Annette Salter, a woman of victory of The Temple of Glory Community Church. Woman of truth and standards. I'm truly blessed to be connected with her.

To Deacon Stacy Staton, Pamela Oglesby and Maurice Gates inspirational writers God placed in my path on this journey. I thank you. My prayer for you is to continue on your journey inspiring others with your truth.

Last but not least, I thank God for my dearest cousin, author, writer, and publisher of my book, Ersula K. Odom, Sula Too LLC. Thank you for your encouragement, inspiration and love through it all. Thank you for the wisdom, knowledge and understanding of an author's journey. May God continue to add to your success!

A Letter to My Readers

Dear Readers,

My writings are based on true stories and events that have happened over the course of my life. The book was written for the sole intent to inspire, give you hope, and heal those broken places in your life.

My stories, poems, and testimonies share heartaches, disappointments, sadness and pain. Offering you the peace of knowing all things are possible when you put God first. Also, know that as long as you have just a little faith you can overcome any obstacles, and be that vessel of love that God has called you to be.

Get to know Him personally, and sit back and watch His works. Know His plan for your life is perfect. We all have our own road to reach eternity. Stay in His presence, keep your mind on Him, and you will have peace within. Always remember your journey is not about you.

Love

Karen

Table of Contents

Foreword

The heart, many believe it is the seat of our emotions; our fears; our wants; our desires...etc.. But, our emotions do not seem to be from our actual physical heart but from our individual, collective and shared, experiences. What matters to me may not matter to you. And so, the journey begins. We find happiness and then sadness. Learning to cope and deal with this ebb and flow of life can be difficult for many. Learning to forgive and love after the pain and disappointment is the test of all tests.

How do we heal the wounds, the bad and/or ugly injuries, those deep gashes in the flesh of our being? *"Healing for the Hurting"*, is one way we can learn. From the journey of another, understanding can be gleaned.

If you are dealing with past and/or present injuries from another or even from oneself, *"Healing for the Hurting"* is the book for you. In this process, learning to be honest with oneself is the beginning of healing. Identifying the hurt is next. Acknowledging one's role within the scheme of things is another.

I am no expert; however, I've had to learn forgiveness, forgiveness of others and myself. We must never forget we are not always the one who has been hurt, but we have hurt others.

If you are seeking a way to regain mastery of your journey, then *"Healing for the Hurting"* is for you. May the door of healing, love and forgiveness be opened to you.

William Stephens

God Said "Make It Plain! Write It, Read It & Run It!"

My vision for my life is the purpose you gave me. Now I know! Now is the time! This book serves as a message to all. It's a book of restoration from life's hurts, discouragements, disappointments, and let downs.

Psalm 30:5 Weeping May endure for a night, but joy (but God) will come in the morning! Habakkuk 2:2 And the Lord answered me, and said, write the vision, and make it plain upon tables, that he may run that reads it.

My Wait Is Over! I shall proclaim my crown! I will walk in your Glory! My time is Now! I'm in my season of preparation for what is to come! For it has come! Thank you, Lord for being my strength and my redeemer!

Proverbs 16:3 Commit thy works unto the LORD, and thy thoughts shall be established.

My life is not my life. My life was meant for you. My works are all done for the Glory of God! My knock downs, my let downs, my tears, and my long sufferings are not in vain. In the mist of confusion, in the mist of the distractions, in the mist of the noise, and in the mist of life happenings God is still in control! He's preparing my way to a greater destiny. For He spoke,

Jeremiah 29:11 For I know the plans I have for you," declares the Lord, "plans to prosper you and not to harm you, plans to give you hope and a future.

What God is doing, what God did, what God has done for me, He will, He shall, He has already done for you.

Hebrews 11:1 Now faith is the substance of things hoped for, the evidence of things not seen.

There is a dark cloud that surrounds you in your storm. You have to gather enough strength to push pass, push through and press on through those clouds. Faith!

Matthew 17:20 And Jesus said unto them, Because of your unbelief: for verily I say unto you, If ye have faith as a grain of mustard seed, ye shall say unto this mountain, Remove hence to yonder place; and it shall be removed; and nothing shall be impossible unto you.

What is a storm? A violent disturbance of the atmosphere with strong winds and usually rain, thunder, lightning, or snow. Storms generally lead to negative impacts on lives and property such as storm surge, heavy rain or snow (causing flooding or road impassibility), lightning, wildfires, and vertical wind shear - Merriam Webster. Results of the aftermath (broken hearts, broken marriages, loss of job, homeless, infertility, betrayal, low self-esteem etc.). What is your storm?

God is not a storm, but storms do remind us that there are forces so much stronger than us. A strong storm is a reminder that we need a God, who is stronger than the storm:

Mark 4:37-41 "*A furious squall came up, and the waves broke over the boat, so that it was nearly swamped. Jesus was in the stern, sleeping on a cushion. The disciples woke him and said to him, 'Teacher, don't you care if we drown?' He got up, rebuked the wind and said to the waves, 'Quiet! Be still!' Then the wind died down and it was completely calm. He said to his disciples, "Why are you so afraid? Do you still have no faith?" They were terrified and asked each other, "Who is this? Even the wind and waves obey him!*

God has given all of us power in the name of Jesus! It's all of to you! You determine your destiny. God is waiting on you! What happens in your life is not the next man's fault! Take responsibility for your choices, action and change of direction. This is the first step to your healing and recovery.

1 Peter 2:24 - *Who his own self bares our sins in his own body on the tree that we, being dead to sins, should live unto righteousness: by whose stripes ye were healed.*

Let the word of The Lord begin your healing process. For we are nothing without Him!

There is calmness after the storm. A sense of peace, love, joy and hope! Our life's journey is going to take us through storms more than once. But the outcome is based on how you cope with the storm. How well were you prepared?

> *Psalms 34:14 Depart from evil, and do good; seek peace, and pursue it.*

All things happen for a reason. In all storms there is peace within. Within knowing that God who's on the inside of you is keeping you, sustaining you and is working on your behalf. I am a living witness. I come to share my testimonies through spiritual, uplifting, unique, self-worth poems and short stories.

"Let the Healing Begin...."
"Love Is the Greatest!"

Ephesians 5-26-27 That he might sanctify and cleanse it with the washing of water by the word, that he might present it to himself a glorious church, not having spot, or wrinkle, or any such thing; but that it should be holy and without blemish"

"Forgiveness"

Healing from within requires forgiveness. Hurt is formed into all shapes and sizes. But when hurt is caused by another's action you have to forgive that person. God says in

> *Ephesians 4:32 Be kind to one another, tender hearted, forgiving one another, as God in Christ forgave you.*

See we often seek God to forgive us of our sins. Our faults and short comings, but forget that it's still a sin not to forgive those that has done us wrong.

> *Matthew 6:14-15 For if you forgive others their trespasses, your Heavenly Father will also forgive you, but if you do not forgive others their trespasses, neither will your Father forgive your trespasses.*

See, this works hand in hand. God expects us to love one another. Love thy neighbor as you love yourself.

"My Testimony"

I've been faced with the challenge of forgiveness on numerous of occasions, but one in particular caught me by surprise. It was so unexpected, so surreal. Betrayal! My heart was crushed, and my world changed in a blink of an eye!

Picking up the pieces after the hurt, crushed pieces and sense of lost. First I prayed and asked God for strength. Then I asked for comfort. God begin to show me who I was and how I can make a difference in my life but more importantly in another's. I began to truly learn the meaning of love and how this would impact my well-being.

Because I asked for God's help, He said He would help me but needed my help in doing so. Faith without works is dead! I wanted the pain to just go away; I didn't want to feel anymore. God said in order for my healing process to take place I had to forgive the one who hurt me.

How could I to do this when the situation seemed so unbearable? Hurt kept being thrown at me by the very same person that hurt me from the beginning. God spoke again and said, "Love." I said, "Yes! I surrender to your will."

So, He began testing of my faith and trust in Him. I was placed in a position to treat this very same person that betrayed me with love. When he spoke with anger; I spoke with love. When he acted out of anger, I acted out of love. At that point he didn't know how to take me. I was not giving him the drama he desired. He grew tried, weary and confused. He broke and began simmering down to where we had some peaceful communications. Now the big test had come. I thought to myself, am I prepared for this? The meeting face to face! I always began my day praying.

Ephesians 6:10-17 The Armor of God
10 Finally, be strong in the Lord in his mighty power. 11 Put on the full armor of God, that you can take your stand against the devil's schemes. 12 For our struggle is not against flesh and blood, but against the rulers, against the authorities, against the powers of this dark world and against the spiritual forces of evil in the heavenly realms. 13 Therefore put on the full armor of God, that when the day of evil comes, you may be able to stand your ground, and after you have done everything, to stand
14 Stand firm then, with the belt of truth buckled around your waist, with the breastplate of righteousness in place, 15 and with your feet fitted

with the readiness that comes from the gospel of peace. 16 In addition to all this, take up the shield of faith, with which you can extinguish all the flaming arrows of the evil one. 17 Take the helmet of salvation and the sword of the Spirit, which is the word of God.

He was kind to me; I was kind to him. I turn quickly, with tears in my eyes and I prayed. I asked God, "Why this way? I can't do this. This is so hard! Treating him with love after all of the hurt!" God then said, "Allow the Holy Spirit that's within you, that I left you to comfort and intercede for you. I'm here with you, I'll never leave you nor forsake you. You're not alone.

I turned back with the biggest smile and continued my walk in love. I forgave him and my heart began to heal. I began to stop dwelling on the hurt and what caused the hurt. Instead, I prayed for him daily.

Matthew 19:26 But Jesus looked at them and said, "With man this is impossible, but with God all things are possible."

Karen Stephens Cooper

"It All Starts With Love"

Someone asked the question, "What's love got to do with it?" My answer: Without love you are nothing!

You are like the wind without the blow
The sun without the shine
The wave without the water

The darkness without the moon
The ice without the sickle
The fire without the flame

The cake without the flour
The bread without the yeast
The child without the guidance

You are lost without the found
The car without the steering wheel
The yoke without the egg
But there is hope, faith and love. The greatest of these
three is Love!

1 Corinthians 13

If I speak in the tongues [a] of men or of angels, but do not have love, I am only a resounding gong or a clanging cymbal. 2 If I have the gift of prophecy and can fathom all mysteries and all knowledge, and if I have a faith that can move mountains, but do not have love, I am nothing.

3 If I give all I possess to the poor and give over my body to hardship that I may boast, but do not have love, I gain nothing.

4 Love is patient, love is kind. It does not envy, it does not boast, it is not proud. 5 It does not dishonor others, it is not self-seeking, it is not easily angered, it keeps no record of wrongs. 6 Love does not delight in evil but rejoices with the truth.

7 It always protects, always trusts, always hopes, and always perseveres.

8 Love never fails. But where there are prophecies, they will cease; where there are tongues, they will be stilled; where there is knowledge, it will pass away.

9 For we know in part and we prophesy in part, 10 but when completeness comes, what is in part disappears. 11 When I was a child, I talked like a

child, I thought like a child, I reasoned like a child. When I became a man, I put the ways of childhood behind me. 12 For now we see only a reflection as in a mirror; then we shall see face to face. Now I know in part; then I shall know fully, even as I am fully known.

13 And now these three remain: faith, hope and love. But the greatest of these is love.

"Food for Your Thoughts"

The Fruits of the Spirit
Sometimes in life we go through a season of transition. This is a process that God allows to happen. We have our ups and downs. It may appear that it's the worst thing that could happen to you. It appears that the pain is so unbearable. Just remember God's plan is perfect.

> *Jeremiah 29:1* For I know the plans I have for you, plans to prosper you, not harm you.

While in the process God is allowing something to change, grow, and be born. Let's examine how God's word could feed us, and make us completely full. Food for your thoughts, the fruits of the spirit. Surviving through your lack of nutrients. The fruits of the spirits are as following: let's eat of His word.

> *Galatians 5:22-23* Love, joy, peace, patience, kindness, goodness, faithfulness, gentleness, and self- control.

Love is the greatest of them all. Love hides a multitude of faults. Love is God.

Joy, the world didn't give it to you and the world can't take it away. Joy is something you choose to have and to keep. It is that unspeakable joy down in your soul.

Peace that surpasses all understanding. Peace brings good to the atmosphere. It's a calmness that fills the air with a sweet aroma.

Patience, wait on the Lord for guidance and answers. Those that wait will reap the reward.

Kindness, kills bitterness, and allows the love to flow. A kind word begets wrath.

Goodness and mercy shall follow. It's good to be good to one another. Love thy neighbor as you love yourself.

Faithfulness of trusting God's word will allow you to activate all of your fruits among his children. Be faithful and true with your actions.

Gentleness can ease the tension and bring on a reassurance of God's presence through you.

Self-control, think before you react. Pray about everything, and don't worry about anything. Be slow to anger, and listen with an open heart.

Are you full yet? Digest these fruits in your spirit and allow them to grow by activating them by first walking in love. Remember, love is the greatest, God is love!

"Heart's Desires"

Psalm 37:4 Delight yourself in the Lord, and he will give you the desires of your heart.

What are your desires? Are they good or evil? Let's start off by defining the heart. The heart is a muscular organ that controls your circularly systems throughout your entire body. The heart is vital to your health and without the pumping action blood can't flow through your body.

The heart also desires. God's word teaches us right from wrong, and good from evil. Above all else the heart of a saint seeks God.

Psalm 119:1-2 Blessed are the undefiled in the way, who walk in the law of the Lord. 2 Blessed are they that keep His testimonies and that seek Him with the whole heart. God warns us against evil doing. Proverbs 4:14-16 Enter not into the path of the wicked, and go not in the way of evil men.15Avoid it, pass not by it, turn from it, and pass away.16 For they sleep not, except they have done mischief, and their sleep is taken away, unless they cause some to fall.

Let your desires be determined by love. Walk in love, think in love, and speak with love. For what's in a man's thoughts will be expressed in his actions and speech. Where is all this stored? In your heart for your heart is your center function. Without it you cannot live, and without God you are nothing. Make the choice today to allow God into your heart, and He will become the center of your life. Your heart's desires will be given to you through grace, mercy, and love.

"My Testimony"

I always had the love for children, and still do. I experienced the loss of a part of me when I was 23 years old. Kaylondra - my first born. I was single and living in the world. I was at that young age of just enjoying life with no worries or cares. I thought I was enjoying life, and I thought life came without worries or cares.

When I first learned I was pregnant. (Yes pregnant and single.) I was happy that I was about to become a mother. I thought I will always have someone to love, and they will always love me. Have you ever felt that way? It was My heart's desire......it began to grow, and it started with love.

On December 6, 1990, I gave birth to my first born not knowing her life would be cut short. I was a mother, and then I wasn't! I was loved, and then it was gone! I thought it was because I wasn't grounded in the word of God. But now knowing, it was his attempt to get my attention. To prepare me for what is to come. She was born with a birth defect, and developed an infection that her little body could not fight off.

She was flown to Augusta Medical College in Augusta, Ga. She lived to be two weeks old. I remember the nurses placing her in a small cardboard box. They allowed us to transport her back home to the funeral home in Savannah, Ga. Once we arrived the funeral directors and personnel all immediately gathered around the car. I stepped out with the box in my hands. I proceeded to hand over the box, and as soon as I released it I felt a part of me leave as well. It felt like I stepped outside of my body. A feeling I would never forget.

Here I was dealing with hurt from the loss of a child. I was clueless but I had the love of others that prayed for me and prayed with me. I found God in the mist of my tears. In the mist of my emotions. In the mist of having a baby outside of marriage! He gave me my heart's desire, and He also gave me life. Yet still in the world God kept me.

Still in the world God never left me. Still in the world He protected me. I realized then that God had a plan, and a purpose for my life. Even though my child was not here with me, I was still a mother. I still could love. I still had love because God was still with me. His seeds were planted and it was all up to me to nurture them and grow them because that's what a mother does.

It was my heart's desire. I married in 1992. Within this union I was pregnant four times, but only have two surviving children. For that person that's reading this right now, and your heart's desire is to become a loving parent. I say don't give up, and don't give in. Keep the faith, and stand knowing God's plan is perfect. I lived through the miscarriages. I lived through the tubular pregnancy.

My fourth and fifth pregnancy was a success of my faith in God, and God's unfailing love. God gave me my heart's desire! My two beautiful girls Kalonna and Carla!

> *Psalm 37:1-40* Fret not yourself because of evildoers; be not envious of wrongdoers! For they will soon fade like the grass and wither like the green herb. Trust in the Lord, and do good; dwell in the land and befriend faithfulness. Delight yourself in the Lord, and he will give you the desires of your heart. Commit your way to the Lord; trust in him, and he will act.

"Being Free"

Being free from the hurt,
Being free from the pain,
Being free from self-destruction.

After the rain comes sunshine,
After the darkness comes light,
After the heartache comes joy!

No matter what has happened in your life to cause hurt, pain, or heartache, healing and being set free can take place. However you have to allow God's unfailing love to manifest in your life. Open your heart, and allow Him in.

1Peter 5:7 Casting all your care upon him; for he careth for you.

Move yourself out of the way! Accept the fact that your life does not belong to you! Your purpose on earth is to do God's will! It's not about you! What you are going through is to prepare you to help the next person, or generation! This is where you will find that unspeakable joy that no man can take away, unless you give it to him!

Philippians 2:4 Let each of you look not only to his interests, but also to the interests of others. Let your works speak for you!

I found in life that all things work together for those who love the Lord! Love is the key to all of life's situations. Learning how to love is a decision, a choice, and sacrifice. A decision to say this is the right thing to do. A choice to say I have chosen to walk by God's commandments, and a sacrifice to save someone's soul.

Galatians 5:13 For you were called to freedom, brothers. Only do not use your freedom as an opportunity for the flesh, but through love serve one another.

"You Are a King and She is Your Queen"

You are the king that God created,
Created to stand strong and firm
He gave you your queen to have and to hold,
To love and cherish with all your heart's concern.

She is your rib, a part of you
Kiss her, caress her, and she will be true.
When she's weak, you are strong,
Your love for her will never do wrong.
You are the King and she is your Queen

Honor her, lift her up for she is your inner you,
The smile on her face, and in her heart, loves you too.
Rise up King and take your throne,
Your Queen is right at your side, you'll never walk alone.
You are the King and she is your Queen

Trust God from the beginning to the end and
All the in between.

Karen Stephens Cooper

"The Tiller, The Blower and The Weights"

Let me start off with defining my title. Let's begin to build the picture......A garden tiller, also known as a plow, is a motorized machine that continuously turns soil with the help of rotating blades. A leaf blower is a gardening tool that propels air out of a nozzle to move yard debris such as leaves. Merriam-Webster

Leaf blowers are typically self-contained handheld units, or backpack mounted units with a handheld wand. Weight training is a common type of strength training for developing the strength and size of skeletal muscles. It uses the weight force of gravity (in the form of weighted bars, dumbbells or weight stacks) to oppose the force generated by muscle through concentric or eccentric contraction. Merriam-Webster

Our life has many different roads we must travel. Twist and turns, that take us through tunnels of life, sounds like the mechanical operation of a garden tiller. It continuously turns using a rotating blade to toss the soil about. Rotating blades tossing about our lives, circumstances, and situations. Then comes the wind, the blower of peace. Peace, that surpasses all understanding, sounds like a leaf blower that moves the debris from around. The debris of lives circumstances and situations.

Now it's time to grow, to rebuild, and be restored from within. To be strengthen within by God's weight training class of His word, sounds like we are about to lift some weights to strengthen us from within. Weights can be a force of a heavy load on our lives, but this weight is God's word rebuilding, restoring, and redirecting our paths.

Psalm 55:22 Cast your cares on the Lord and he will sustain you; he will never let the righteous be shaken.

"When Life Throws You An Unexpected Test!"

Our journey in life is a road of joy, love, pain and sorrow. One minute you are up, the next minute you are down! Sometimes not understanding the changes. The changes are our seasons in life. Life is not a fairy tale as the young girl imagines.

Have you ever been head over heels in love with someone? I heard someone say that love can make you blind, cripple, and crazy! Wow! What a mouth full.
True love doesn't hurt, nor does it take from you. I say this to the young ladies reading this right now, know your value! Love should never have you blind, cripple or crazy. However in life when you're given that unexpected test, and you're not prepared for it. Ouch! That hurts!

Here I stand in love with hurt. You asked the question, hurt? How can you be in love with hurt? When you settle for less than you deserve. When the fist becomes your sense of comfort. Thinking he must love me, or he wouldn't have tried to teach me better. See, you chastise your child to teach them right from wrong. But the Bible does not state you chastise your mate to teach them right from wrong!

Young, low self-esteem and not knowing the meaning of true love. Not prepared for the test. I want to help the next young lady that is in a relationship that is filled with hurt. Ask yourself these questions. Do I love myself? Look in the mirror. Do you like what you see?

> *Psalm 139:14* *I will give thanks to You, for I am fearfully and wonderfully made. Wonderful are Your works, and my soul knows it very well.*

Remember these words that God has spoken. First step in learning how to love you. Let's prepare for our test.
I once was sitting in the emergency room hearing the doctor say one more hit, and you will not have live to tell it! I thank God He had a plan, and a purpose for my life. Someone was not so blessed. He saw favor, and He saw life.

> *Jeremiah 29:11* *For I know the plans I have for you," declares the Lord, "plans to prosper you and not to harm you, plans to give you hope and a future. Now that's true love!*

My road to recovery, my road to deliverance, and my road to self-worth was some years to come. In the mix of all of my heartache and pain, God showed me He was still there. I began to pray more, and seek His face. Although I didn't know His word as I should, I learned to trust God with my life.

Proverbs 3:5-6 *"Trust in the LORD with all your heart, and lean not on your own understanding; in all your ways acknowledge Him, and He shall direct your paths."*

There was years of physical abuse and affairs. Hurt after hurt. I began to grow tired. I began to want a better life for my daughters, and myself. All eyes on mommy. I asked myself what am I teaching my children? What are they learning? I began to love myself for the sake of my daughters. That's true love. God doesn't want you to suffer by the hands of another.

John 10:10 *The thief comes only to steal and kill and destroy. I came that they may have life and have it abundantly.*

I spoke of being delivered. Yes, I had to be delivered from man! Why? Because the love that I thought was true love was toxic! I left, and went back several times. I was blind, cripple, and crazy! But God delivered me from man! See, when you give up something, but you have not been delivered from it, you are bound to fall for it again. However, once you are delivered you are set free!

2 Corinthians 1:10 *Who delivered us from so great a death, and doth deliver: in whom we trust that he will yet deliver us.*

Karen Stephens Cooper

"My Love"

My love for you is more than you could imagine
My love for you is more precious than silver and gold
My love for you is everlasting, and breathe taking
My love for you is like the beginning with no ending

My love for you is peace that surpasses all
understanding
My love for you is my grace and mercy
My love for you is all that you need
I am God, your all and all; my love for you is for real

"Grateful Tears"

After the pain, comes joy!

> *Nehemiah 8:10 Nehemiah said, "Go and enjoy choice food and sweet drinks, and send some to those who have nothing prepared. This day is holy to our Lord. Do not grieve, for the joy of the Lord is your strength."*

Tears of hurt, anger, and despair will be overcome with tears of gratefulness! Stop, look, and listen to your heart. God is speaking right now. Don't allow the enemy to steal your joy.

When we speak of the enemy we picture a person that has hurt us. The enemy my friend, is not a person. It's a spiritual wickedness that will dwell where it's welcome. It will use your spouse, children, friends or any person who comes in contact with you.

I come to tell you don't allow the attacks of the enemy to take, or destroy your walk of love. You must forgive those that have hurt you in order for you to heal. In this process you will begin to see the works of the Lord working on your behalf. Grateful tears.

Karen Stephens Cooper

"I'm Lost Without Words"

As I stand in awe, I'm lost without words.....
As the tears began to flow, I'm lost without words....
As I question why? I'm lost without words....
As I wonder how the story is going to end, I'm lost
without words....

Then I remembered my help....
Then I remembered my protector.....
Then I remembered my healer.....
Then I remembered my God, Jehovah Jireh, my
provider!

It began to happen, my faith, my trust
It began to happen, my peace, my love
It began to happen, my strength, my joy
It began to happen, I'm lost without words, but I'm
found in my praise!

"Through It All"

Sitting here and thinking back. I value every breath I take. Through it all God has kept, protected, and provided. My faith in God is built on trust, honor, and truth. Through it all I could not have made it this far without Him. This journey to where I am today was not easy. It's still a test of my belief in Him, but because I know Him personally and have experienced His presence in my life it makes my journey so well worth it.

You may be questioning where is God in your life or why did He allow this pain that seems so unbearable to enter your life? Has He forgotten about you? How much longer God? - (before He answers your prayers). Why God? Why?

You're sitting there with tears in your eyes. Hurt feels like a brick weighing you down. Your head is hurting. Your heart is crushed. You don't know what your next step should be. You feel like you are drowning. You feel like taking your last breath. You have lost all hope.

But God! Through it all, He hasn't forgotten. He hears your cry. He's carrying 90% of your pain. He knows how much you can bare. Take a moment and just breath, sit quietly, and listen carefully. He's been trying to speak with you. Say this prayer:" My Lord give me eyes to see your greatness in my life, ears to hear you speak so gently to my heart, and a tongue to sing your praise, because through it all you have been keeping me. Lord give me strength, wisdom, knowledge, and understanding. Lord I seek your face. Show me you and renew my heart. Create in me a clean spirit. Amen"

"My Testimony"

A hot summer night. July 16th, 2003 at 2:30 a.m., I was awakened from a peaceful dream by a ringing telephone. I answered as if I was fully awake. I heard my mama's voice say I need you to come over. I immediately got up, and got my girls without any hesitation and went. I already knew what my mama was going to tell me because he came to me in my dreams. His big smile, and bright eyes, he said "I'm riding high now. "

I can still see the vision of my dream. I had to look up high as he spoke to me clothed in white. I miss my baby brother. Taken from this world by the hands of another. About 3:00 p.m. earlier that day I had my last conversation with my baby brother. He was so happy I literally felt his happiness through the phone. He had called me at work to tell me thank you for helping him get his car out of the shop. He was without his car for about a month. So that explained why he was so excited, thankful, and happy. Many people came to me after learning of his death that came in contact with him that day. They all shared how happy he was on that day. In the course of 12 hours his joyous spirit came in contact with so many.

44

Through it all God gave me strength to help plan his funeral, write and print his obituaries, and to be strong for my family most of all, my mama. My brother and I were really close in spite of the 14 year difference. He was my shadow as he grew. He was like my own child. When he became a young man we were each other's ace boom. I cried often in private for God allowed me my time to mourn. I still cry, but not often and it's a cry of just missing him.

Although my heart ached from losing him by the hands of another, I have forgiven those that were involved. Even though to this day his murder is unsolved. I prayed for them, and asked God to forgive them and help me heal. That's when it all began; my tears were becoming laughter after I remembered all of our good times. My tears became a smile when I felt his presence with me. He'll forever live in my heart.

This is for the person reading this right now that has experienced the loss of a love one that you were truly connected. The tears will lessen. Your heart will heal. The pain will become bearable, and when you think about them you will be able to smile because of the beautiful memories you have shared. Through it all I survived and I know you will too. Trust God's plans and know He's in the mist of all things. The Bible says in

Proverbs 3:5 Trust in the LORD with all your heart and lean not on your own understanding.

Dealing with death no matter how you have lost that person, or how long that person has been in your life is still hard. The pain of losing someone so close to you is the same. I lost my first born, and the pain was unbearable. I also lost my baby brother, the pain was unbearable, my father, unbearable pain, my oldest sister and another brother, the pain felt unbearable, but God made me stronger, enough to bare it all. When there's a connection so strong, rather by kin or friendship, the pain of death is unbearable.

To you, trust God and believe you too will be healed from the hurt. Your memories will make your heart smile, something no one or thing can take from you. Their presence will always be with you, deeply embedded in your heart. God is able, and is always true through it all!

Karen Stephens Cooper

"My Baby Brother"

He was my baby at heart
He was an inspiration to others
My baby brother
His dream was to create unity
For all to become as one
My baby brother
Here he wrote it
Here I speak it
My baby brother
From his heart he speaks
Through me he is heard
My baby brother
He's gone, but not forgotten
His dream and vision lives on
My baby brother..........
Love you Jonta, My baby brother

"God's Divine Mistakes"

Broken marriages, relationships, friendships....I'm not perfect. Mommy mistakes, family issues, self-destructions......I'm not perfect. Have you ever heard of "Perfect Patti"? Well I'm not her. Mirror, mirror on the wall....I'm not perfect.

Mistakes are intended to be made. God is intentional.... Wrong choices could be a road to success, only if you learned something along the way. God's divine mistakes were designed, predestined, and willed out for my life.. Don't ever let anyone speak as if they know you better than you know yourself. Mirror, mirror on the wall....I'm not perfect.

In the mist of my journey I picked up some goodies along the way, and tucked them in my heart. I'm learning the true meaning of love. Yes, still learning because as long as you are breathing there is room for learning and growth. Remember I'm not perfect..... God's divine mistakes.

The true Biblical meaning of love is how we act and treat one another.

> *1 Corinthians 13:4-7 New International Version (NIV)4Love is patient, love is kind. It does not envy, it does not boast, it is not proud.5It does not dishonor others, it is not self-seeking, it is not*

easily angered, keeps no record of wrongs. 6 Love does not delight in evil rejoices with the truth. 7 It always protects, always trusts, always hopes, and always perseveres.

Patience in life is so important, and yet very trying. With all of life's issues, mistakes, and just everyday coping with today's society, it can be hard. I'm not perfect - road rage, short tempered - God's divine mistakes. Lessons, though some learned, I am still learning how to master patience, but it is tucked in my heart, and it is maturing. Being kind to one another helps with growing your patience for we all have issues, mistakes, short comings that we face daily.

So smile, or give a hug just because of God's love growing inside of you. Allow it to manifest into something beautiful.

"My Testimony"

I'm not perfect. When I was developing a closer relationship with God and I did not understand a circumstance or situation, I asked God for wisdom, knowledge, and understanding. I have learned you have to pray for discernment. You can't share your testimonies with everyone. Haters are real. Envy is dancing all around you, and can be closer than you know.

However, the Bible says love does not envy. I rejoice with you in your gladness, and that's not at all hard for me to do. I'm not perfect....so being me thinking everyone feels the same is God's divine mistakes.

My heart speaks when sharing my testimonies, or asked, "How did you do or make it?" I share the goodness of God in my life. How He has made a way! How He has kept me! How He has made provisions for me, and my girls! How everything I have, and achieved is all because of God! I'm nothing without Him! So I don't boast, because I think I'm better than you. The God I serve, and know can do the same for you and more! I boast IN the Lord and He gets all the Glory!

Love doesn't dishonor others, not self-seeking and not easily angered. I will be the first to admit I'm not perfect. I know I have hurt others along the way. I know I did some things for attention – in the wrong way. I know my temperament, and I know me better than you do, but God knew me first. God's divine mistakes.

We learn, we correct, and we do better. There's room in the house (heart) to do more, so let's get our house in order. Confession is good for the soul. I love you always no matter what....forgive me...I'm not perfect.

I can truly say I thank God for a forgiving heart....I'm not perfect. A brief testimony; I have been in conversations and been asked the questions "well what was it I said to you that offended or hurt you? What did I do so to you? "I was sitting there thinking with a blank look." Well that's what I thought, nothing you can't remember! "

Then, I was questioning myself, wondering if I'm I the crazy one! I'm not perfect, so I went to God, as I have learned to do over the years, and found out one of the goodies I thought I had picked up along the way, was already tucked and snugged nicely in my heart. "Love keeps no records" once I forgave you I let go. I can still remember the pain in a positive way, because it has taught me valuable lessons. I choose to take the lessons to help others. Intentional, divine mistakes. Designed, predestined and willed.

Love doesn't delight in evil, but rejoices in truth. Along my journey I'm grabbing hold of honesty, trustworthy, loyalty and goodness. Learning how not to gossip, judge or cause harm can be a challenge for some. I'm not perfect, but the key to walking in love is truth. Be true to yourself! Respect others, and respect will be given to you. Treat others like you would want to be treated. Offer a hand to help someone that is down, and rejoice with them about the goodness of God. Speak truth into their situation, comfort them with the word of God.

Now I'm all packed, and my heart is full. With many cracks and bandages that reads as such (protects, trust, hope and preserve). I love completely with my heart. I've been broken, knocked down, and knocked out! However, through it all, God has kept, strengthened, and carried me. I know the pain of being used, abused, and talked about while feeling in despair. God gave me protection, faith, hope, and life. So by being true to myself I have no choice, but to walk in love, and give back those goodies God has nicely tucked in my heart.

I thank God for His divine mistakes along my life journey. Mirror, mirror on the wall...I'm not perfect.....

Psalm 139:14 I praise you. I am fearfully and wonderfully made; works are wonderful, know that full well.

"Hidden Secrets"
"Forgiven"

As I sit here and put deepest thoughts on paper, tears are streaming down my face. My deepest embedded feelings are being released. It's been over twenty-five years since I was first taught forgiveness, and what it was all about. With my emotions tossed aside, I was made too love. Being blamed for actions of another, the scars were being healed from the outside in. Hidden secrets...Forgiven!

It was a night of horror. A night I'll never forget. A night of protection. A night I first held onto God's hands. Out and about living it up in the world, and kicking it on the dance floor. Oh boy was I having a good time for such a brief moment. Then the clock quickly fast forwarded. It was just like turning a light switch on and off.

The music was jamming, laughter was in the air, and all of a sudden out of nowhere confrontation arose. Quickly we exited the club with thoughts to avoid trouble, and just to get home. As we began to ride past another club we decided to pop in, and see if we liked the spot. Nope it wasn't us, so we quickly hurried back to my car and proceeded home. This only took us about five minutes. Within those five minutes it gave us time to drive into the trouble we thought we left behind.

While we were pulling up to my friend's home she asked me to drive around front. Frantically, she exited my car and proceeded around the back of my car. Then all of a sudden, I heard commotion. I heard screams and then gun shots. As I looked in my mirror, I could see her being beaten, and then the gun turning towards me. I quickly hit the gas as I heard the shots being fired. I was so scared and just wanted to get home. I drove as fast as I could.

When I ran into my mom's house I found her sitting in her room on the phone. I was screaming "Call 911 she's being beaten and he's coming for me! He has a gun mama!" With all the commotion, my oldest sister ran into my mom's bedroom. I grabbed the phone and dialed 911.

My mother by then was at the front door trying to keep him from entering, but It didn't work. He entered. My sister closed the bedroom door to try and keep him out. He was coming for me! I'm on the phone screaming he's going to kill me! He knocked the room door down! It landed on my leg. I thought I was shot! All I heard was gunshots, and a voice speaking to me don't hang up the phone, hold on.

When I think back on that moment, after it was all over, I know it was God saying don't let my hand go. Hold on, I got you! There were three bullets found in my mother's room. I was sitting on her bed holding the phone which was God's hand. The bullets that were fired entered her headboard, mattress, and wall. Remember the door struck my leg. I thought I was shot. My sister said she stood by him and was screaming "no" as she kept hitting at his hand as he fired the shots. All at close range, we were in my mom's bedroom (8x10).

God had a protective shield around me as long as I held onto His hand. It felt like I was in a box, with a shield around me and the sounds were muffled.

The next day I looked at my car, and it was a dreary day for me. There were three bullet holes in my car. One entered the door of my gas tank, the other two into my trunk. God had me in His hands even before I knew I needed to grab hold of His. Six bullets were fired by someone so close to me. Someone I loved all my life, and to this day I love my brother.

I was taught how to forgive, and keep love flowing. My mom wasn't going to allow this to cause a separation among her children. I was there for my brother, as he was held accountable for his actions. He was also shot and wounded that very same night. The next day I was at his hospital bedside. I have been by his side from that day until today and he is forgiven. I love my brother no matter what. Hidden secrets, and yes time heals and scares are covered, wounds are mended.

Hidden secrets. When I really think back on this moment, which occurs less frequently now, tears still flow. Healing outside in, and I was made to love, and taught to forgive. A choice I made, out of respect for my mom's authority. God allows things to happen all for a reason. God can change a person. My brother a kindhearted, and humble man today. When I'm in his presence I feel safe. Now that's God!!
Forgiveness is hard to do for some, but it's a must for your own soul. Forgiving someone can be difficult. Why do we need to forgive others? How can we forgive a

person? The Bible can provide us with answers, inspiration and direction.

> *Mark 11:25 "And when ye stand praying, forgive, if ye have fought against any: that your Father also which is in heaven may forgive you your trespasses."*

I was never asked how I was doing, dealing or coping with that situation. I always had to put the best on the outside. Somethings are just meant to be in secret between you and God until the time is right. Healing outside inward.

You can heal from your deepest hurts. Those deep secrets that are hidden within. God is able; He heals the broken-hearted and broken spirits. Hold on He has you! I know that I'll never let go!

"Shared Tears"

It was winter 2005, the year God blessed my girls and me with a home. My friends and I were sitting around His breakfast bar, remembering life lessons. We laugh, we cried and we gave God His glory! For we knew all that we were and all that we had was because of God. All that we owned was His.

Sometimes in life we find ourselves in a battle, broken marriages, financial issues, family problems, or just discovering who we really are through these situations. It was a beautiful sunny winter Saturday, as we sat in the kitchen around the breakfast bar.

The sun gleaming slightly through the window. One after the other we began to reminisce on where God had brought us from. We talked about some of our deepest hurts, and disappointments. We shared tears of sadness, and joy. We encouraged each other without skipping a beat, acknowledging God in the mist of every circumstance.

This moment impacted our lives because it was truly genuine. Until this day, every now and then we find ourselves reminiscing about that day. True friends, and shared tears, are good for the soul. Like that old saying, sometimes family is not by blood.

We each have dealt with so many other issues since then, but one thing we know is we have a stronger shoulder to cry on if needed. Shared tears in many ways are a release to regain strength. I thank God for that beautiful sunny winter Saturday, but most of all the shared tears.

"Shattered Pieces"

Having a personal relationship with God and trusting His plan for my life is perfect, and has opened up many doors. Praying for wisdom, knowledge, and understanding has been given to me with a heart of discernment. Have you ever felt as if your heart was just ripped out of your body? Have you ever felt shocked about an outcome? Just totally caught by surprise? Left only with shattered pieces - now what?

Discernment dictionary meaning: ability to judge well. "An astonishing lack of discernment". In Christian contexts - perception in the absence of judgment with a view to obtaining spiritual direction and understanding. "without providing for a time of healing and discernment, there will be no hope of living through this present moment without a shattering of our common life."

I'm in AWE as I write this in hopes of helping others who are hurting, and trying to pick up the pieces. The title, and message/testimony I'm about to share. I look at the spiritual meaning (healing and discernment) and (shattering of common life). Right at this very moment I know it was nothing but God that has placed this special piece on my heart to share. A divine connection by having that personal relationship with Him! Hallelujah!

My story, my testimony: God can speak to us in our dreams, which are visions. I have been given this gift to foresee certain things. I'm still learning interpretation of some of them, but have accepted this ability as having a heart of discernment.

Shattered Pieces - where do I begin? I had a dream, and I was shown a vision. A week went by, and I had the same dream, the same vision.

I knew at that moment the enemy was lurking. I again had the dream with the same vision. I recalled speaking with one of my sisters briefly about it, because it was disturbing. She said be careful. I prayed and I asked God in the mist of my troubles to give me strength to be able to handle whatever it is that is about to rise up against me. God gave me a scripture:

> *Isaiah 54:17* *No weapon formed against you shall prosper, and every tongue which against you in judgment you shall condemn. This heritage of the servants of the, and their righteousness Me," Says the Lord.*

When you can feel an unclean spirit, that's discernment. Satan can and will use anyone if you allow him to use you. This is spiritual warfare. That's why only God can fight for you. Walking in love can be hard, but it's a choice that has to be taken. It's a must in order to survive in this cruel world. When you fall short of this (shattered pieces) you ask for forgiveness and move on, and do better.

Here I am, standing in awe of an outcome, that at the end of that day, was unnecessary. Emotions arose. Hurt words were said. Actions were not of God. I was not at all surprised of the storm that was circling me, because I had foreseen it already. I was prepared in strength, but was caught off just a little of who was in this circle. Shattered pieces, but a valuable lesson learned. Now how do you cope with picking up the pieces?

Like broken glass, you carefully pick up the pieces in hopes not to get cut or cut again. Like mending a perfect picture back together, but the cracks and lines are still visible. Like learning how to forgive, but can't forget. Shattered pieces, a heart with many patches, but filled with so much love. That's why it's so important to learn to love because it will take you through all of life's hurtful lessons.

I'm in your presence, but it not the same,
I rebuke Satan, in Jesus name.
Shattered Pieces, broken glass.
Healing within, hurt a thing of the past.
Picking up, mending together.
Love is all I have, I'm doing better.
Shattered Pieces, broken glass.
God lives in me, my love shall last.

No matter what has caused your heart to be heavy, turn it all over to God. He heals the hurting.
Psalm 34:18 118 The Lord close the broken hearted and saves those who are crushed in spirit.

Pray for discernment and it shall direct your path.

"The Love, The Soul and The Experience"

Captivating....Love. Motivating....Soul. The Experience of God's presence. Laying in a fetal position, your world just turned upside down, and you don't know what you're going to do. Your back is up against a wall, and you're in a world wind. Tears are flowing, and you begin to pray...that's all you know, and that is more than enough.

Captivating ....you begin to feel strength. You feel His presence. You hear His voice "I'm here with you, you are loved, I love you and long for your soul. You're beautiful, you're wonderfully made, and you're mine." "Grab my hand, walk with me, and listen carefully as I speak truth to your heart." I love everything about you, your flaws I see you only as a rose bud with thorns that are slowly opening into a beautiful rose." You are marvelous, and you're built with strength. Walk with your head held high, and your stride with grace and your smile as beautiful as you are." I love you...you can rest in me, let me hold you ever so gently." Feel my presence, feel my touch, I long for your love, draw nearer to me." I love your smell, every hair on your head, and the mold of your body and... You're beautiful. I love you." "You're as white as snow in My Eyes."

Motivating.....you're standing, you're breathing again and you're glowing. "My child you were made to love. Stand knowing you're covered. Stand knowing you are strong, Stand knowing you are courageous, and stand knowing I am God! The beginning and the end. I speak life into your situation, I speak life into your very being, and I speak life into your soul. My life I speak is love. Slowly breathe in and out, and allow my presence to saturate into your soul.

Divine energy, I speak life, and inner beauty into your soul. I speak life, and your soul cried out Hallelujah! Your essence is beautiful. I dwell within you. You're victorious because I am fighting your battle. You're powerful because I have given you all power through my word. Your very soul, your identity is undeniably marvelous."

The Experience..... I'm in awe of your presence my Lord. You have saved me! I'm beautiful, wonderfully and marvelously made! I'm free from bondage, self-destruction, and man-made wounds. Oh, how awesome the experience of learning how to walk with you, talk with you, and love like you. The experience is beautiful, awesome, and magnificent, just as you are my Lord. Thank you for wisdom, knowledge, and understanding. Thank you for inner strength, beauty, and love. Thank you for the lovable, soulful, and the breathtaking experience! I was broken, mended, and healed.

Kalonna, Karen & Carla

"God's Love"

As I lay here in bed with only the sounds of my oldest daughter. It's quiet, she is sleeping and grinding her teeth.

I can feel my baby daughter kicking me in my back.
I think what a joy to be touched by Angels.
Then a thought came to my mind, and I said to myself,
I finally know what love is.

Love is when you're feeling sad, and God gives joy!
Love is when you're feeling weary, and God gives you peace!
Love is when you're feeling weak, and God gives you strength!

Love is when your friends leave your side, and God gives you comfort!
Love is when your heart is heavy with burdens, and God gives you hope!

Love is when your life is just in shambles. and you seem to be in total darkness,
and God gives you light!
Love is when your enemies are rising up against you, and God gives you shelter!

Love is God. When He comes along and cleans all that
mess up!
"God is Love"

My heart, and my soul cries out "Oh how I love the way
I'm being loved!
It's not man's love. No, it's God's Love!
Now that's Love!

Karen Stephens Cooper

"Peace, Joy and Happiness"

Those days of abuse, misuse, and abandonment are
gone
No more, I'm free, I'm home!

Peace, joy, and happiness is what I've always prayed for
I have it now, it's mine and I adore!

Many nights I cried,
Many days I tried,
So many times I just wanted to hide

Peace, joy, and happiness is what I've always prayed for
I have it now, it's mine and I adore!

You were supposed to be my friend
My friend to the end
You were supposed to protect me
Not neglect me

Peace, joy, and happiness is what I've always prayed for
I have it now, it's mine and I adore!

Yours hands were made to touch me gently
Not to abuse me mentally, and physically
Your feet were made to walk near to me
Not to stomp me until I couldn't see

Peace, joy, and happiness is what I've always prayed for
I have it now, it's mine and I adore!
That's just a little of what I've dealt with

Healing for the Hurting

It's rises as high as a cliff
So much more, more than more
I thank God, like an eagle I can soar

Peace, joy, and happiness is what I've always prayed for
I have it now, it's mine and I adore!

Now my child is what my God has spoken to me
You've prayed, struggled, and survived the hands of he
Come draw near to Thee and let Me set you free
Giving you peace, joy, and happiness
It's yours for you to keep.

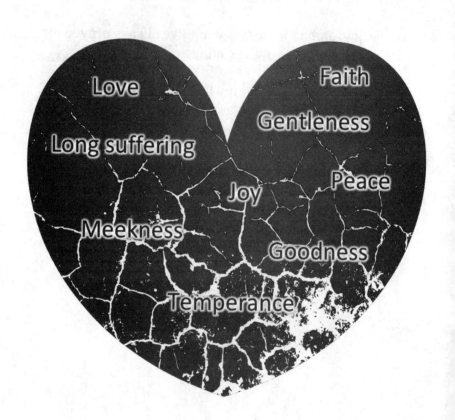

"Being Who I Am"

Being who I am is a simple task.
Letting go of any negative energy, and producing
positive vibes.

Being who I am is what the doctor has ordered.
Loving, giving, caring, and sharing.

Being who I am is God's greatest love.
Praying, praising, and giving glory to the man above.

Being who I am, I'm who I am.
Love, joy, and happiness.
God's love.

Note to the readers: Stay true to yourself. Love yourself
and let no man steal your joy.
Know your self-worth, and to whom you belong. God
has created you out of love.
Walk in love, breathe love, and live love. You are who
you are. Embrace you.

"Your Seasons of Life"

As your life spins in a circle, it's creating seasons in your life. Seasons of hurts, hope, love, and healing. Seasons of disappointments, truth, faith, and forgiveness. Seasons of pain, encouragements, beliefs and peace.

It is spring, the birds are singing. The flowers are blooming. There's love in the air. Your world seems so perfect. You're happy.

Summer time the heat is on. Vacation time, family fun, and games. Your life seems so at peace.

Leaves began to turn. Fall is here. Things are seemingly spinning out of control. Despair is knocking on your door. You're so caught so off guard.

It's cold in the winter. Trees are dying, winter appears lonely. You're left with no hope. Feeling so incomplete. Feeling lost with no signs of life.

You begin to remember how God has kept, delivered, and provided for you. You see hope, peace, and your faith begin to grow. Here it is springtime again. As your life revolves, you're given many opportunities to learn from God. His goodness, grace, and mercy allows life obstacles to test us of our faith in Him. Learn of His word which speaks truth in our lives. This makes you a believer in His works knowing all things work together for those who love the Lord.

"My Testimony"

Sharing some of my personal stories with you has shown me a lot about myself. Thinking on those things that seem so devastating at that time. It was painful, heartbreaking, and nearly life ending. The pain is no longer there when I remember. My heart is at peace because I have forgiven. This is what the Bible teaches us, to learn how to forgive and forget. You may not forget what happened, but you'll heal because the pain has been forgotten. This has allowed me to share, inspire, and give hope.

"Forgive me Lord of my trespasses as you forgive those that have trespassed against me." When you forgive yourself and others, God will forgive you. When you've completely healed, you'll forget the pain. Forgive and Forget. Remembering the story is your testimony. There is good in every circumstance and even situations.

These are quotes from my dearest friends who have given me the inspiration, and motivation to write. Your life should always be a testimony of God's works.

* "Girl you make the struggle look good!" LOL
* "Karen, you just being you. Just being honest when shared. Just knowing what you been through, and you'll still standing. You make it seem so easy."
* "I admire you because you are a go getter, you don't let anyone and anything keep you down. You're so strong."
* "Girl, here I am trying to give you words of comfort and you'll bless me by encouraging me!"

Not bragging or boasting, because I was at awe when these words were spoken. Listening as they shared how I made them feel, made me want to cry on the inside but I also knew that is was God who deserved the praise, and I silently thanked him.

I believed a Christian life should be an open book. How would you hear of God's greatness? How would you be inspired? Truth, hope, belief, and faith. Never boasting about myself, just boasting about God's grace and mercy in my seasons of life.

1 Corinthians 1:31 Therefore, as it is written: "Let the one who boasts, boast in the Lord."

"It's O.K. - It's Opportunity-Kindness"

It's O.K. when you're face with anger
It's O.K. when you're talked about
It's O.K. when you're left behind

When opportunity knocks, open your heart with kindness

It's O.K. when things don't seem to go your way
It's O.K. when your back is up against a wall
It's O.K. when you're running out of time

When opportunity knocks,
open your heart with kindness
Just say to yourself when you're feeling in despair
that it's O.K.

Then when given opportunities,
act out of kindness toward someone else.
This will give you a sense of joy to make others happy
in spite of your current situation.
Your current situation then seems O.K.

My baby girl tells me all the time when she can tell something's on my mind, or I'm about to speak my mind. She says mommy it's O.K. This always seems to calm me, and now I understand why. Opportunity-Kindness. God's work is needed.

"Tips on Healing"

I learned to forgive
I learned to trust God
I studied His words
I wrote down scriptures that pertained to my situations at that time.
I meditated on God's word
I listened to string music which is music of healing
I found a quiet place to talk with God
I began to stray away from negativity and tried to think positive
I learned that there is good in every circumstance
I often spoke with my spiritual mothers whom were of God and spoke wisdom into my life
My circle of friends and activities changed
I used the hurt in my life to gain access to survival
I learned if you believed in things you shall have
My faith grew because I believed in truth
I held on to hope knowing things would get better
I encouraged myself
I gave when I didn't have, I made sacrifices to help others
I smiled when I felt like crying
I prayed in secret
I learned of true love and activated it
I stopped worrying over things, and people I had no control over
I began to let go of things and allowed God to do His works.

Sure, none of this was easy. None done all at once. It all was a learning process, and the outcome was an awesome experience.

I was getting to know God personally. When God shows His face in your life you are completely unaware how or when. So, when it happens, you are so in awe of His presence, so full of joy when you feel how much He loves you. It's still hard at times, but when I think back on what He has brought me through it gives me hope to hold on.

Patience is virtuous, and God's love for you is real. I am still learning, and trusting God's word. Still a work in process, but a better person than who I was yesterday. After all, it's not at all about me, but why I am here on earth. My purpose is to do the works of God, spread His goodness, and walk in Love. Always remember we are His vessels.

"Meditational Scriptures for Healing"

Prayer has healing powers. Always remember to pray

Psalms 73:26 My flesh and my heart may fail, but God is the strength of my heart and my portion forever.

Isaiah 41:10 fear not, for I am with you; be not dismayed, for I am your God; I will strengthen you, I will help you, I will uphold you with my righteous right hand.

Matthew 11:28-30 Come to me, all who labor and are heavy laden, and I will give you rest. Take my yoke upon you, and learn from me, for I am gentle and lowly in heart, and you will find rest for your souls. For my yoke is easy, and my burden is light."

John 14:27 Peace I leave with you; my peace I give to you. Not as the world gives do I give to you. Let not your hearts be troubled, neither let them be afraid.

2 Corinthians 12:9 But he said to me, "My grace is sufficient for you, for my power is made perfect in weakness." Therefore I will boast all the more gladly of my weaknesses, so that the power of Christ may rest upon me.

Psalms 55:22 Cast your burden on the LORD, and he will sustain you; he will never permit the righteous to be moved.

Psalms 107:20 He sent out his word and healed them, and delivered them from their destruction.

Psalms 147:3 He heals the brokenhearted and binds up their wounds.

Proverbs 3:5-6 Trust in the LORD with all your heart, and do not lean on your own understanding. In all your ways acknowledge him, and he will make straight your paths.

1 Peter 2:24 He himself bore our sins in his body on the tree, that we might die to sin and live to righteousness. By his wounds you have been healed.

1 Peter 4:19 Therefore let those who suffer according to God's will entrust their souls to a faithful Creator while doing good.

Isaiah 43:18 Remember not the former things, nor consider the things of old.

Mark 11:23 Truly, I say to you, whoever says to this mountain, 'Be taken up and thrown into the sea,' and does not doubt in his heart, but believes that what he says will come to pass, it will be done for him.

Romans 5:1-2 Therefore, since we have been justified by faith, we have peace with God through our Lord Jesus Christ. Through him we have also obtained access by faith into this grace in which we stand, and we rejoice in hope of the glory of God.

Romans 8:28 And we know that for those who love God all things work together for good, for those who are called according to his purpose.

1 Corinthians 13:7 Love bears all things, believes all things, hopes all things, endures all things.

2 Corinthians 5:6-7 So we are always of good courage. We know that while we are at home in the body we are away from the Lord, for we walk by faith, not by sight.

Philippians 3:13-14 Brothers, I do not consider that I have made it my own. But one thing I do: forgetting what lies behind and straining forward to what lies ahead, I press on toward the goal for the prize of the upward call of God in Christ Jesus.

Hebrews 11:1 (KJV) Now faith is the substance of things hoped for, the evidence of things not seen.

Revelation 21:3-4 And I heard a loud voice from the throne saying, "Behold, the dwelling place of God is with man. He will dwell with them, and they will be his people, and God himself will be with them as their God. He will wipe away every tear from their eyes, and death shall be no more, neither shall there be mourning, nor crying, nor pain anymore, for the former things have passed away."

"Thankful"

I'm sitting here with a sense of peace. I'm so thankful for life. For the very air I breathe. I'm thankful for where my journey in life has brought me, and I'm so excited for what the future holds. I've learned that life is not a fairytale, and that it's a road of ups and downs. However I'm so thankful. Thankful for the God that I serve because of who He is.

Thankful for everything I have, and everything I am. I'm thankful for you, and what God is going to do in your life. Just trust Him, and lean not to your understanding, but acknowledge Him in all things. I'm thankful for His grace, mercy, and His unfailing love.

I know He's watching over me. I'm so thankful for the level of faith I have in God. Thankful for the place where I can trust Him. When going through situations in life I'm thankful I have a different perspective on things, allowing the positive impact to overcome the negative.

I know you may be dealing with something right now that has your heart hurting. It's not easy to wipe away the tears, or to hold your head high. It's not easy to get up, and keep going. It's not easy to sleep at night. It's not easy to smile. It's not easy to be thankful, and to continue to give God praise in spite of what you're dealing with. Remember there is power in prayer, and it may not seem easy to pray. Just repeat these words, "Lord help me." Yes, it's just that easy to talk with God! "Lord I need you."

Prayer is your communication with God. He's waiting to hear from you.

I'm thankful, that God is fixing it right now for you. I'm thankful that you're feeling your help coming. I'm thankful that the sun is beginning to shine in your life. I'm so thankful for that smile that sense of peace, and joy that has you truly thankful right now! In Jesus name let it go, and let God. Hold on to His unchanging hand and share the love.

Lord, thank you for saving me. Thank you for entrusting me to share your love through my stories, poems, and testimonies. Thank you Lord for loving me, in spite of me. I'm so thankful. I love you Lord. For it's not about me, it's to do your will.

Thessalonians 5:18, "Give thanks in all circumstances, for this is God's will for you in Christ Jesus."

Psalm 30:5 "*Weeping may endure for a night, but joy cometh in the morning.*"

My name is Karen Cooper. God has allowed me to survive through the storms, rise above circumstances and situations so that I can share my testimonies. Testimonies of faith, love and peace. I come to give you words of encouragement, truth and hope. I share my life journey to let you know you are never alone. God is with you every breath you take. He desires only one thing from you. That is to stay in His presence. Keep your mind focused on Him. Your faith lies in all you believe. Believe in your heart that you have the victory because your end has already been foretold. Give God the praise for all things and in all things, praise God. Your heart is the core of your very existence. God lives within. He heals the brokenhearted. Above all else, guard your heart, for everything you do flows from it. Proverbs 4:23.

I'm from Savannah, Georgia and now reside in Effingham County. I have an Associate Degree in Accounting with over 20 years of work experience. I'm a single mother of two daughters, Kalonna & Carla, who are college students. I love the Lord. I am on a mission to do His will. I'm a member of The Temple of Glory Community Church under the awesome leadership of Dr. Matthew M. Odum, Sr. I enjoy writing, sharing my thoughts through words of experience, truth and wisdom. I thank God for His hands on my life. His plans for my future.

My daily prayer is always asking God to show me where I'm needed, in order for Him to get the Glory. Allow me to shower His love among His children knowing the Glory belongs to Him. Use me, this imperfect being, to spread His love by doing what He has call all of us to do. Love one another.